YOU ARE THE MAGIC: YOU JUST DON'T KNOW IT YET

Short Book - Endless Possibilities

SEAN JENSEN

Acknowledgements and References
Some teachings and concepts in this book are inspired by the works of various thought leaders, including Bashar (channeled by Darryl Anka). I would like to acknowledge their contributions to the collective wisdom that has shaped this journey. For further exploration of Bashar's teachings, visit *www.bashar.org*.

First Edition
Ebook: 979-8-9918966-8-9
Print: 979-8-9918966-2-7
Cover Design by Damonza

Printed in the United States of America

"Knowledge isn't free. You have to pay attention."

—Richard P. Feynman

Table of Contents

My intention for this book is to awaken the parts of you that may have been forgotten but that your soul has always known.

I want to remind you of the immense love and power within, and that the answers you seek are already inside you, waiting to be rediscovered.

This book offers a short, impactful journey—something you can absorb quickly and begin applying immediately to unlock your highest potential.

The knowledge and insights I've gathered throughout my life now serve as a guiding light, empowering you to step fully into your true self and embrace the wisdom that has always been within you.

1
The Blueprint of Life

To MOVE FORWARD in our understanding, we must first grasp the fundamental aspects of the experience we call "life." The idea is that we are all souls that are from the spiritual realm who have chosen to experience life in a physical form, aiming to learn and to expand our consciousness.

Our higher self has outlined a blueprint, or contracts, for each life we live, filled with different lessons designed for evolution as souls. This concept aligns with the common notion of "destiny".

While we may not always remember what our higher mind has planned, it doesn't mean we lack the free will to alter our journey. The higher contracts determine the lessons we are meant to learn, but our free will shapes the choices we make at every moment, influencing the circumstances of our growth.

Have you ever pondered why certain challenges arise in your life? Remember, the choice is always yours to make, empowering you to shape your own path and destiny.

Self-awareness is the starting point of all self-development.

Before you can change or improve anything in your life, you must first know where you are. Self-awareness is the key to understanding your thoughts, beliefs, and emotions. It's the foundation upon which you can build a life of intention, growth, and alignment with your highest self.

"Knowing yourself is the beginning of all wisdom."

—ARISTOTLE.

The more you become aware of who you are—your patterns, strengths, and areas for growth—the more empowered you are to make conscious changes that align with the life you truly desire. Self-awareness opens the door to transformation.

2
You are Your World

Many people believe that we are souls who came *into* this world to experience the Universe. But there's a deeper understanding that can shift your entire perception of existence:

The Universe is consciousness. And you are consciousness.

You are not separate from the Universe—you are a piece of it, experiencing itself through an individual perspective. Everything and everyone you observe is a projection of your own consciousness.

You are the world.

You can think of this through the lens of the commonly known simulation theory, which suggests that reality is not as fixed as we might believe. In truth, everything you experience is a reflection of your inner world—your thoughts, beliefs, and emotions.

This means that the people and situations in your life are not random. They are mirrors, reflecting different parts of you. No one has power over your reality because it is your "Youniverse"—a personal creation of your consciousness.

You may wonder, *But what about the other people in my life?*

Everyone you encounter is a reflection of a version of themselves that you have agreed to interact with in your experience. On a higher soul level, their souls have agreed to play a role in your life for the evolution of your soul.

There are no accidents.

If someone cuts you off in traffic, on a soul level, they've agreed to help you learn a lesson—perhaps in patience or maintaining peace. Every experience serves a purpose for your growth.

Picture it like each of us wearing virtual reality headsets in the void. We are all experiencing different realities, yet in your world, you are always the main character. This is why life is always happening *for you*, not *to you*. It is the very nature of your existence.

Life unfolds from the inside out.

"As you are, so is the world."

—Ramana Maharshi

3
Alignment

True alignment with your highest good, with Source, and with the Universe is never something you have to force. When you're in alignment, everything flows effortlessly to you, like a river that knows its course.

Forcing is not alignment.

When you are on a path that resonates with your deepest truth, life unfolds with ease. The people, opportunities, and resources you need will naturally come your way. You won't need to struggle, stress, or overextend yourself. Instead of feeling like hard work, it will feel like play—a joyful expression of your authentic self.

On the other hand, notice when you find yourself pushing too hard, forcing outcomes, or struggling against the current. If something requires excessive effort and drains your energy, it might be a sign that it's not in alignment with your true path, or that the timing isn't right.

Listen to the moments when you feel frustrated or depleted. These situations often reveal what you need to let go of, creating space for the path of least resistance—one that serves your highest purpose and supports your well-being. Alignment allows you to move through life as your most authentic self, with a sense of ease and joy.

Prioritize relaxation. When you're relaxed, things flow. It is effortless.

Remember: relaxation is a sign of alignment.

The more I relax, the more I receive.

4
Nothing Happens by Chance

There are no coincidences or accidents in life. Everything is divinely orchestrated by the Universe. It all unfolds in perfect timing, even if it doesn't always match your current desires or expectations. From a higher perspective, beyond our immediate likes and dislikes, everything is happening for the evolution of your soul.

Remember, life is happening for you, not to you.

You might not fully understand why certain events unfold the way they do, and that's okay—that's part of the journey. Instead of resisting, allow yourself to get curious!

Ask yourself: Why is this happening? How might this be benefiting me?

As you explore these questions, you'll begin to see the synchronicities and hidden patterns that guide your path. These signs and events are not random; they are the Universe's way of leading you towards your highest good.

Nothing happens by chance; there's a purpose behind every event.

5
Embrace the Unknown

The unknown is a realm of endless possibilities, miracles, blessings, and synchronicities.

The answer to uncertainty isn't found in the search for certainty; it lies in self-trust.

Surrender to the unknown—not as a loss of control, but as a declaration that your highest self is always guiding you.

It's this understanding that liberates you from the grip of 'what ifs,' doubts, and fears. Embrace uncertainty with open arms and release your need for control, allowing your heart to welcome new experiences.

Remember, miracles can only exist in the space of the unknown. Knowing every detail, like reading the entire script of a movie before watching it, would strip the magic from the experience.

Find the excitement in not knowing what comes

next! You are the author of your life's journey, and you designed it long before you arrived here.

Uncertainty and the unknown are woven into the fabric of life. Embracing them is the gateway to life's magic, inviting you to uncover the wonders that await.

**Miracles don't happen in the known,
miracles happen in the unknown.**

6
Reframing Your Perspective

Perspective changes everything.

How you choose to see the world shapes your reality.

See it differently.

Say it differently.

It's not a loss—it's a new beginning.

It's not anxiety—it's excitement.

Think of it like a photographer capturing the same scene from different angles. Every shot tells a different story, even though the subject is the same. You have the same power: the ability to shift your perspective and discover the hidden positives in any situation. Because there is always something positive.

Reframing your thoughts isn't about denial; it's about empowerment. It gives you the ability to reclaim control, to choose how to interpret your experiences, and to move forward with clarity and strength.

"Our key to transforming anything lies in our ability to reframe it."

—Marianne Williamson

7
What Are Your Beliefs?

What you say to yourself matters.

Your belief system matters.

Positive beliefs propel you forward, helping you live life to its fullest. Affirmations, when aligned with these beliefs, become a powerful tool for reinforcing thoughts that serve your growth and well-being.

But just as important, if not more so, is recognizing the beliefs that hold you back—the limiting beliefs that prevent you from reaching your true potential. Many of us carry these hidden thoughts, which shape our mental patterns and influence the words we speak. And as we'll explore in later chapters, the words you speak have a powerful impact. Your beliefs form the foundation of your thoughts, which ultimately direct your actions and shape your immediate circumstances.

It's easy to see how deeply these beliefs impact your life because your outer world is a reflection of your inner thoughts and imagination.

No matter how strong your positive beliefs are, if you're still holding onto limiting ones, they will weigh you down. Imagine a powerful car with an upgraded engine—it won't reach its full speed if it's towing a heavy trailer behind it. To truly accelerate, you need to let go of the baggage.

Limiting beliefs often crumble under scrutiny. You have to ask yourself: why do you believe this? For example, one might think financial freedom is impossible because they're stuck in a dead-end job with bills piling up. But why isn't financial freedom possible for you? You may not see how it could happen right now, but if others have achieved it, why can't you? Or you might think it's hard for you to lose weight. Why is it hard for you? If others can achieve a healthy, strong body, why can't you? These limiting beliefs always seem to provide "reasons" for why they're true, but ultimately, you have the power to stop believing them. And when you realize you don't have to accept them, you grant yourself the freedom to start your transformation.

Becoming aware of these limiting beliefs is essential. When you change what you believe, you change what you think—and when you change your thoughts, you allow inspirations and inspired actions to emerge, ultimately transforming your reality.

You are Divinely Guided, Supported, and Loved.

You are worthy of every blessing.

You are worthy of every desire in your heart.

Freedom is your birthright.

Abundance is your birthright.

You are the creator of your life.

8
Self-Acceptance

We've explored the idea that you are your world and that everything you experience is a reflection of a part of you. How you see yourself shapes not just your inner world but also your outer reality.

We all carry the weight of past mistakes, regrets, and the times we didn't meet our own expectations. It's easy to be harsh on ourselves, to dwell on the moments where we feel we fell short or didn't do enough. We might criticize ourselves for the "should haves" and "could haves" that linger in our minds.

You're not alone in feeling this way. We've all been there.

But for you to step into the version of yourself that lives the life you dream of, you must be willing to release the aspects of your old self that no longer align with your growth. Think of a caterpillar—it doesn't cling to its form but willingly surrenders to the process of becoming a butterfly.

Self-acceptance means embracing who you are right now, in this journey of becoming.

You don't need the world to accept you.

You need to accept yourself.

If everything around you is a projection of your imagination, then how you see yourself is the most powerful force that shapes your reality.

Your beliefs about yourself influence how others perceive you.

If you don't accept yourself, how can you expect others to? If you don't love yourself, how can others find that love within you?

The acceptance you seek must first come from within. The love you desire starts with you.

The love you've been looking for has always been right there—in the depths of your own heart.

The love you seek is already within you.

"To be beautiful means to be yourself.
You don't need to be accepted by others.
You need to accept yourself."

—Thich Nhat Hanh

9
The Meaning of Life

Many of us spend our lives searching for the meaning of life, hoping to uncover our true purpose.

The truth is, you are the one who assigns meaning to your life. Life itself is a never-ending journey of growth and transformation. Your soul chose to experience this life, to learn, and to evolve. And this journey of learning is infinite; there is no final destination to reach, only an endless unfolding of experiences.

Every moment presents an opportunity to learn and grow. Instead of asking, "Why is this happening to me?" try shifting your perspective to, "What is this teaching me?"

The meaning you choose to give to each situation—whether it's positive or negative—shapes how you experience its impact in your life.

- Negative meaning in, negative effect out.

- Positive meaning in, positive effect out.

The Universal language that transcends all understanding is love. Whatever you do, do it from a place of love, not for love. Let your passions and excitement guide you toward a purposeful life, one that you co-create with the Universe in alignment with your true self.

**Every moment is an opportunity
to learn and explore.**

10
Peace

Peace is not the absence of noise, mess, or trouble; it's the acceptance of it all—the ability to simply be.

It comes from an inner knowing that all is well.

You are safe, here in this moment. In every moment. No need to rush. No need to stress. No need to dwell on the past or worry about the future.

Peace is being here and now, in the present moment.

Reconnect to the present by becoming aware of your breath.

The past is behind you, and the future has yet to unfold. But deep down, you know it will unfold perfectly.

So take a breath, right here.

All you need to do is come back to this moment. Everything you need exists in the here and now.

"The only Zen you find on top of a mountain is the Zen you bring with you."

—Zen Proverb

Here's a quote from Thich Nhat Hanh on **"Being".**

"We have a tendency to think in terms of doing and not in terms of being.

We think that when we are not doing anything, we are wasting our time.

But that is not true.

Our time is first of all for us to be.

To be what?

To be alive, to be peaceful, to be joyful, to be loving.

And that is what the world needs most.

We all need to train ourselves in our way of being, and that is the ground for all action.

The quality of our being determine the quality of our doing."

—Thich Nhat Hanh

11
Your Self-Worth Shapes Your Reality

Your self-worth doesn't just affect your wealth—it influences every aspect of your life.

You accept the love you think you deserve. You receive what you believe you're worthy of.

Even if your conscious mind knows you're worthy, your wounded inner child might still be carrying unhealed wounds.

Many of us have experienced mishaps or trauma, particularly in childhood. That child doesn't disappear. He or she still resides within you, influencing your sense of worth.

It's important to realize that we carry beliefs that may no longer serve us. Perhaps you had strict parents who never gave you the encouragement you needed. Maybe your father never told you he was proud of you. Or you grew up in a toxic, abusive environment where physical affection and safety were missing.

We all carry different wounds. These experiences may have taught your inner child that you weren't worthy of love, praise, or affection.

Get to know your inner child. You might try looking into a mirror and speaking directly to that part of you.

Your adult self may already know, "I am loved." But your inner child needs to hear, "You are loved." "You are safe." "You are worthy of love." "You deserve all that your heart desires."

The Universe gives you what you believe you're worthy of receiving. Many people struggle to manifest their desires because, deep down, they don't truly believe they deserve them.

A limiting belief might sound like, "That's too expensive for me," or "That's not for someone like me." But this is *your* world. You can have, do, or be anything you want. There are no limits—except the ones you place on yourself.

So catch yourself when you hold back because of a limiting belief. Realizing it's a false belief isn't the start of the process; it's the end. Once you see it for what it is, you're free from its grip. That's it!

Removing limiting beliefs that hold you back is just as important as remembering your inner power to create the life of your dreams.

Your internal self-talk matters.

12
Remember Who You Are

What is your true nature beyond all the conditioned beliefs?

You didn't leave unconditional love to come to Earth; you have simply forgotten your connection to it. The essence of Source energy, the Universal force that binds us all, is love.

Your soul, your consciousness, is a fragment of the Source, experiencing itself from a unique, individual perspective. Many of us have endured traumas and hurts that may have masked our connection to Source—to love. But the truth is, the love never left us. Just because we cannot see or feel it from our current perspective doesn't mean it isn't there.

To reconnect with this love, you only need to look within. If you seek, you shall find.

As we discussed earlier about the blueprint of your life, there are aspects that are your destiny—your passions and talents, the unique gifts that make you special. No one else can do what you do in exactly the way you do it.

As Amy Catania so beautifully expressed, "This life you've been given is not to appease the world around you, but to express the world within you."

> **"You often feel tired, not because you've done too much, but because you've done too little of what sparks a light in you."**
>
> — Alexander Den Heijer

It is your birthright to know that you are here for a reason. Despite all the challenges, the ups and downs, and the moments that seem like failure, know that you have always been there for yourself. Failure is merely an incomplete picture. It's not the end of your journey; it's the beginning of your success story.

All you need to do is be your authentic self. As Carl Jung said, "The privilege of a lifetime is to become who you truly are."

May you awaken to the creative power within you, enabling you to live a purposeful, meaningful life that radiates love and light to everyone you encounter. In the words of Bashar, "We all have the same life purpose: to be yourself as fully as you can, in the best way you know how."

In tender stillness, you discover, you are love.

13
Intuition: Your Inner Guide

We cannot talk about your inner power without mentioning your intuition—your gut feeling, your sixth sense, or whatever term resonates with you.

In earlier chapters, we discussed how your higher self has set sail on this journey to experience life in a physical body, with you as your world. Your higher mind knows the plans and challenges laid out for your physical self, but you, as the physical mind, are here to live out this journey without the higher realm's memory.

As Bashar teaches, imagine your higher mind as standing on top of a mountain, clearly seeing the bigger picture and guiding you, the physical mind, through the valley. While you may face uncertainty, doubt, or fear from your limited view, your higher mind never does, because it created the blueprint.

This is what intuition truly is: the voice of your higher

mind. We've been taught to rely on the physical mind to figure out how things should happen, but your higher self sees beyond the limits of space and time. As Bashar says, "It is not your physical mind's job to conceive how things will happen. You are here to perceive how things happened."

Let go of the need to control how things unfold. You are not alone in this; your physical mind is just one part of you. Your higher self is an extension of you, and you must learn to trust yourself.

People often talk about their gut feeling, that sense of whether something feels right or off. It's true—your intuition is your ultimate guide, steering you toward what aligns with your highest good.

So, listen to that inner voice—the one that speaks with love and never judges. This is your higher self. Be discerning when thoughts arise; intrusive thoughts from negative energies are not your true self. By connecting more often with your intuition, you'll become familiar with its voice. It will lead you toward alignment and liberation. Life becomes much lighter when you trust in the guidance that was always meant to carry you.

"Intuition is the whisper of the soul."

– Jiddu Krishnamurti

14
You Are Constantly Transforming

You are not the same person you were a moment ago. As Bashar teaches, you are becoming a different person billions of times every second. In every moment, you are shifting, evolving, and transforming into a new version of yourself.

This understanding changes everything. It's not about learning how to change—it's about realizing that you are already in a state of constant change, continuously stepping into a different reality with each breath, each thought, and each choice. It's like you're hopping into a new reality, a new timeline, in every moment.

This means you are free from the limitations of your past. Who you were yesterday, or even a moment ago, does not define who you can be right now. You hold the power to redefine yourself in every instant, shaping your life based on your highest vision and truest desires.

Your greatest power lies in your ability to choose who you prefer to be, regardless of anyone else's expectations or opinions. You are the creator of your own "Youniverse," the master of your own journey.

Quantum mechanics reveals that all possibilities exist simultaneously—every potential timeline and reality is available to you. By choosing to focus on the version of yourself you most desire to be, you can shift into the reality that aligns with that vision. Embrace this power to transform, and know that in every moment, you are becoming the person you were always meant to be.

"No man ever steps in the same river twice. For it's not the same river and he's not the same man."

– Heraclitus

15
Look Back and Be Proud of How Far You've Come

It's easy to get caught up in what's still ahead—focused on the next goal, the next achievement, the horizon that always seems just a little further away.

And that's okay. It's okay to have big dreams. It's okay to reach for more.

But it's also okay if you're not there yet. It's okay to be exactly where you are right now.

Pause for a moment. Take a deep breath. Reflect on the journey you've traveled.

Think of all the challenges you've faced, the growth you've experienced, and the strength you've shown. You've come so far. You've stood by yourself through it all. You've been your own source of support, courage, and perseverance.

You are here today, not by accident, but because of everything you've done to get to this point.

Before you look ahead to the next milestone, give yourself the recognition you deserve. Look back.

And be truly proud of how far you've come.

You are exactly where you need to be. And from here, you will rise even higher.

You are never behind because you are on your own journey.

16
Everything is Energy. Energy is Everything.

It's often said that spirituality isn't rooted in science, but that simply isn't true. In fact, many spiritual concepts align closely with scientific principles and can be observed, experimented on, and repeated.

One of the core principles is that everything in the universe is energy. Traditional physics tells us that all physical matter is made up of atoms.

But what are atoms made of?

Protons, electrons, and neutrons.

And what are those made of?

Quantum physics reveals that these particles, and everything composed of atoms, are fundamentally energy—existing as unique frequencies and vibrations that shape the material world.

As Nikola Tesla once said:

"If you want to find the secrets of the universe, think in terms of energy, frequency, and vibration."

If everything is energy, then any change in matter must begin with a shift in energy—through frequencies and vibrations. No one can create change without first changing their energy.

When you shift your energy, you change your life.

Understanding this is key to harnessing your power and shaping your reality.

Be the energy you want to attract!

17
Bashar's 5 Facts that Exist in Creation

Bashar, channeled by Darryl Anka, has shared five core facts that he believes to be the fundamental principles of existence. According to him, these facts are the unchanging truths of creation, while everything else is fluid—shaped by perspectives, opinions, and beliefs. Let's explore these five facts:

1. **You exist.**
   This fact is the simplest yet most profound truth: your existence is undeniable. No matter what experiences or challenges you go through, the very fact that you are conscious, that you are alive, is a miracle in itself. This acknowledgment can be a powerful reminder of your inherent value and the infinite possibilities that lie within you.

2. **Everything is here and now.**
   The past, present, and future all exist in this

moment, here and now. This idea emphasizes the importance of presence and mindfulness. The energy you put out in the present moment is what shapes your experiences. By focusing your attention on the now, you tap into the true power of creation and manifestation.

3. **The one is all, the all is one.**
   This principle speaks to the interconnectedness of all things. We are all individual expressions of the same universal consciousness. What happens to one affects the whole, and what happens in the whole affects each individual. When you understand this, you see that your actions, thoughts, and intentions have a ripple effect that influences not just your life, but the world around you.

4. **What you put out is what you get back.**
   This concept aligns with the law of attraction: the energy, thoughts, and emotions you project into the world come back to you in some form. If you put out positivity, kindness, and love, you're more likely to receive that in return. This fact encourages us to take responsibility for the energy we bring

into any situation, knowing it will ultimately shape our experiences.

5. **Everything changes except the laws.** Change is the only constant in life, but the fundamental principles of existence—like these five facts—remain the same. Understanding that the laws of creation are unchanging gives us a solid foundation on which to build our lives. It also helps us embrace change as a natural part of growth, knowing that while circumstances may shift, the core truths stay the same.

Bashar points out that everything outside of these five facts is not absolute; they are perspectives, opinions, or beliefs that can be changed. You have the power to alter your perceptions, shift your beliefs, and transform your reality in ways that align with your highest version of yourself.

This understanding reminds us that we are not limited by our current circumstances or conditioned beliefs. We are limitless beings, capable of transforming our lives by changing the way we see the world and our place within it.

"Your life does not get better by chance; it gets better by change."

—Jim Rohn

18
Spiritual Hygiene

You now understand that everything in life is energy, and that there are both positive and negative forms of energy.

Some energies and vibrations uplift and support you, while others can drain or hinder you.

While cultivating positive energy within and around you is essential, it's equally crucial to develop the awareness to recognize negative energies and learn how to clear them to reduce their impact on your life.

Have you ever spent time with someone who constantly complains, only to feel completely drained afterward? Conversations centered on negativity can lower your vibration, leaving you feeling depleted.

Negative energy can have a significant impact on your well-being if you don't know how to protect yourself. One of the simplest ways to clear negative energy is through water—whether it's a refreshing shower or a calming bath in natural bodies of water like the ocean. There are also traditional practices for cleansing energy, such as burning sage or palo santo wood, which are known for their purifying properties. Certain crystals, like black tourmaline or amethyst, are also known to help protect you from negative energies. While we won't dive into all the specific practices, the key idea is that maintaining good energetic hygiene is essential. It directly influences your vibrational state, which in turn affects what you attract into your life.

This concept of energetic hygiene isn't commonly known, and many people may simply label themselves as unlucky when, in fact, they could have lingering negative energies and limiting beliefs around them.

Here's a simple affirmation to practice daily, ideally before you go to sleep: Place your hand on your heart and say, 'I now release any negative energy from my heart and replace it with love.'

Understanding and managing your energy empowers you to tap into your inner strength and create a protective shield against negativity.

19
The Power of Your Perspective

Your perspective shapes your reality.

Because your reality is created by how you see it.

No one else sees the world through your eyes. You are the only one experiencing life from your unique viewpoint. Your perspective *is* your world.

It acts as a lens through which you interpret everything around you. Each thought, belief, and emotion shapes how you perceive your surroundings, creating your personal reality. This means that reality is not fixed; it's a projection of your imagination, colored by your interpretations and reactions.

By shifting your perspective, you can transform your reality, revealing new possibilities and insights. When you understand that your world is shaped by your viewpoint, you are empowered to take control of your experience and consciously create a life that aligns with your true desires.

"There's no power in the world, other than the power that you give to things. All power is within you."

—Abraham Hicks

20
The Power of Your Thoughts

What you think about, you bring about.

Your thoughts are powerful—they generate electric signals in your brain, sending vibrations out into the Universe.

By becoming aware of your thoughts, you can consciously choose what you project, directly influencing your physical reality and attracting what you desire. It's similar to tuning a radio: when you switch from one frequency to another, you expect to hear a different station. Likewise, when you change your thoughts—your frequency—you should expect to experience a different reality.

The principle is simple:

What you think about, you bring about.

The Universe responds to your focus without judgment, delivering experiences aligned with your thoughts, whether they are positive or negative.

That's why it's crucial to be mindful of your thinking. The Universe doesn't distinguish between what you want and what you don't want—it simply mirrors back the energy you emit. By cultivating positive, empowering thoughts, you open yourself to the abundance you wish to attract.

The quality of your thoughts determines the quality of your life.

21
What You Speak Matters

3 Words to Avoid

Our thoughts create our reality, and our words give form to those thoughts. The language we use can either empower or limit us. Here are three common phrases to avoid and what to say instead:

1. **"I hope"**

   "I hope" carries an underlying tone of doubt and lack. It comes from a place of deprivation and vulnerability, suggesting that you don't believe what you desire is already yours. It implies you aren't fully aligned with the belief that you're deserving of your dreams.

   What to say instead:

   Change "I hope" to "I know."

   - "I know I am worthy of wealth and abundance."
   - "I know I deserve this money."

- "I know I have the ability to be successful."
- This shift replaces uncertainty with confidence and empowers you to align with your desires.

2. **"I need"**

   "I need" stems from a place of lack. When you focus on needing something, you are focusing on the absence of it in your life, which reinforces that state of lack. Remember, the energy you put out is the energy you attract.

   What to say instead:

   Use phrases like "I attract" or "I welcome."

   - "I attract opportunities for growth."
   - "I welcome love, abundance, and success into my life."

3. **"I cannot"**

   When you say "I cannot," you reinforce a limiting belief. Whatever you believe internally reflects outwardly in your reality. When you tell yourself you can't do something, you block yourself from even attempting it, creating a self-fulfilling prophecy.

   What to say instead:

   Replace "I cannot" with "I can" or "I am capable."

- "I can achieve my goals."
- "I am capable of creating the life I desire."
- This simple shift opens you up to possibilities and aligns you with the energy of action and empowerment.

"I must become that which I say I am."

—Rev Ike

22
Attention and Flow

You can master your mind by becoming aware of where you direct your attention.

Wherever your attention goes, your energy flows.

What you focus on, expands.

Just as it's essential to be mindful of your thoughts, it's equally important to be aware of where you're placing your attention. When you pay attention to something, you're "paying" for it—essentially "buying" that experience. In other words, you attract what you focus on.

This understanding is transformative because it means the outside world no longer happens to you. Instead, you hold the power to choose where you direct your focus, empowering yourself to shape what manifests in your life.

It quickly becomes clear that concentrating on

negative news or fear-driven narratives does not serve your highest good. Be mindful of what you read, watch and listen to, as these things shape your perception and energy.

Try to take a moment each day to notice where your thoughts naturally drift. Are they focused on things that uplift you, or do they dwell on worries and doubts? Awareness is the first step to reclaiming your power.

Choose wisely where you place your focus, and take charge of your life by becoming the conscious creator of your reality.

Whatever you focus on, the Universe brings you more of that.

"Your attention to it, invites it"

—Abraham Hicks

23
Your Feeling is Your State

A remarkable thing happens when you allow yourself to truly feel.

Often, we become so caught up in the tasks of daily life that we forget to check in with our emotions.

How are you feeling right now?

It's essential to be aware of your feelings because they serve as indicators of your current vibrational state. Your emotional state reflects the vibrations you're emitting.

When you're feeling good, you're in a high vibrational state, aligned with your highest self and the flow of the Universe. On the other hand, emotions like anxiety and fear signal misalignment, reflecting lower vibrations. In these moments, it's important to shift towards a better-feeling thought or activity.

There are many ways to shift your emotional state.

Since your feelings are directly influenced by your thoughts and focus, you can change how you feel by changing what you think about or where you direct your attention.

Physical movement, such as exercising or simply going for a walk, is a great way to boost your mood by releasing endorphins. Laughing is one of the quickest ways to shift into a joyful state—watching comedies or engaging in something that makes you laugh can instantly raise your vibration. On the contrary, consuming content that induces fear, such as horror, can lower your vibration and create a state that may not serve you.

As we've discussed before, relaxation is alignment. Since everything is always working out in your favor, simply relax!

Feeling good is a sign that you're aligning with the Universe, allowing everything to flow effortlessly.

So, tune into your emotions regularly and use them as a guide to check whether you're in alignment.

Feel good, in as many ways as possible.

"Reach for the thought that feels better!"

—Abraham Hicks

**“I do not have to be perfect or know it all.
I just have to feel good right now.”**

—Abraham Hicks

24
Feeling is the Secret

Everything you've ever wanted isn't really about the material object, achievement, or title itself. It's about how you *feel* once you have it.

We all have dreams, goals, and ambitions—visions of what we want to achieve. But more than the actual things, it's the feelings associated with those accomplishments that drive us. It's the sense of fulfillment, joy, pride, freedom, or peace we feel when we've reached the top of our mountain.

The secret to creating and manifesting anything you desire is to feel as though you have already attained it. You must embody the emotions you would experience if your dream were already a reality.

Take a moment now. Close your eyes, and think of one desire you have. Feel the joy, pride, excitement, or peace as if you already have it.

Hold onto that feeling, as if it were your present reality.

When you're in this elevated state of vibration, the Universe can't contradict the energy you're emitting. Instead, it aligns with your vibration, bringing your desires into your experience.

Many teachers suggest techniques like creating a vision board or visualizing what you want from a first-person perspective. These are helpful tools, but the most essential part of manifesting is feeling the emotions you would have if your dream had already come true.

Feel as if you're already in the best health.

Feel as if you already have the ideal relationship.

Feel as if you've already landed your dream job.

Feel as if you already have the wealth and freedom you desire.

It's not about waiting for these things to arrive before feeling good. It's about feeling good now, and allowing the Universe to bring your reality into alignment with that feeling.

Rest assured that your positive feelings are much more powerful than negative ones. Therefore, don't be hard on yourself if you find yourself dwelling on thoughts that make you feel bad. The duality of existence means that both positive and negative experiences exist, and it's natural to go through moments or feelings that we do not prefer. It is by experiencing what you do not prefer that you gain insights into the experiences that you do prefer.

Staying in a state of negativity will continue to attract more negative experiences. Your task, therefore, is to transform those bad feelings into positive ones as best as you can.

"Your work is to consume your now with the thought that feels the best."

—Abraham Hicks

25
Happiness and Gratitude

Happiness is often something that we all pursue as some sort of life goal, as though it is something to be attained.

Happiness is not something you can chase; it does not depend on your circumstances.

Happiness is a state in which you feel good. It is a state that you choose to be in.

How do you feel good? Sure, by following your passion and excitement. It is equally important to be mindful and to be anchored in the present moment. It is often the small things in life that you notice which bring the greatest joy. While it is crucial to know where you are heading in the future, the present moment is all you have, so be in it. Be here.

"The more you slow down, the faster you go."
—Erica Bracken

Start practicing mindfulness in the present moment by taking pauses in your daily routine. Next time, before you rush to the next destination, meeting, or task, take a moment to look around you and listen to the sounds. There is so much beauty to be appreciated in these still moments. It is these moments that improve the quality of your life. Remember, enjoying the journey is just as important as arriving at the destination. As you embrace the present moment, remember the wisdom in the words of Ralph Waldo Emerson: **"Life is a journey, not a destination."**

Gratitude is one of the highest vibrations you could put yourself in. In every moment, there is always something positive. Make it a habit to notice and appreciate the positives in your everyday life. By focusing on what you already have and appreciating it, not only do you raise your vibrational frequency into a state that makes you feel good, but you are also inviting the Universe to bring more of these positive things and experiences into your life.

One powerful tool to practice is when you first wake up in the morning, think of three things you're grateful for, and allow yourself to truly feel the appreciation in your heart. It's not just about recognizing these things in your mind; it's about experiencing the feeling of gratitude. By doing so, you start your day with the vibration of gratitude.

> *"How you start your day is how you live your day. How you live your day is how you live your life."*
>
> —Louise Hay

Happiness is when you're in flow and alignment. To be in this state, as we've discussed earlier, is to make the choice to be disciplined within our inner world and surrender to and trust the Universe.

I am grateful for the abundance that surrounds me, and I welcome more into my life.

26
Surrender and Flow: Focus on Attracting, Not Chasing

True attraction is effortless.

When you attract everything you desire, there is no longer a need to chase anything because you can do, have or be anything you want.

You are always attracting everything in your reality. As we discussed earlier, your thoughts and focus determine what you're attracting. Whether you are aware of it or not, the law of attraction is always at work.

When you decide on your desire, many of us were taught to do all kinds of work to chase that thing, to make it happen. We were always trying to do something to make it a reality.

But what if it could all be effortless? This doesn't mean you simply decide on your desire and passively wait for it to arrive. Actions are certainly required, at least to a certain degree. There is a visual representation that perfectly illustrates the balance between discipline, surrender, and flow.

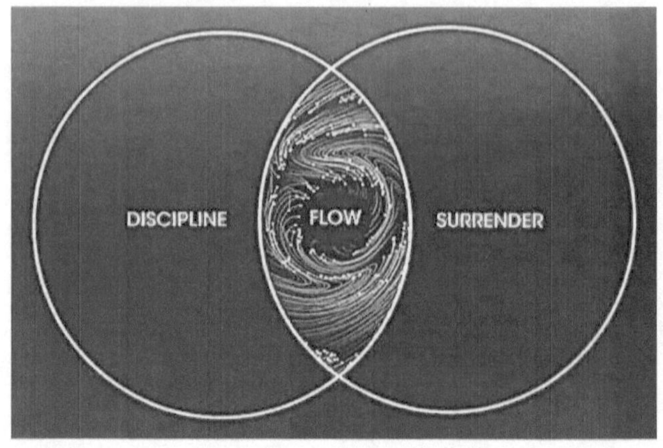

"Concept adapted from widely available sources on discipline, flow, and surrender."

As discussed in earlier chapters, it is essential to cultivate discipline in the quality of your thoughts, intentions, emotions, and in unraveling your limiting beliefs, followed by aligned actions. Your actions will become far more efficient when you take the time to align with the Universe before proceeding.

How do you know if you're aligned? When you feel good and relaxed, you're aligned. Your work is to feel good before taking any action. Once you're in alignment, you will be guided to take inspired actions. To recognize which actions to take, listen to your excitement and passion—they are your guiding clues.

Be mindful of your vibration, the way you feel, before you start anything.

To achieve flow, the other side of the equation is to surrender. Surrendering, as we've mentioned, is not about giving up control but trusting that your highest self has your back and that everything is indeed in control, working out in your favor exactly as it should. It's about allowing things to unfold naturally, without forcing or resisting. Therefore, take action with no insistence or assumptions about how the outcome is supposed to be.

Don't stress over whether you're making the right decision or not. There is no right or wrong. Whatever decisions you make, the Universe works around them to bring you a series of possibilities that shift with your thoughts, feelings and actions. Allow things to unfold even better than what you have imagined.

When you follow this blueprint in everything you do, you are liberated from the worries of whether you're taking the correct steps or not. You will always be taking actions that align with what excites you, keeping you in a state of joy, excitement and passion.

No matter the outcome, trust that it will always benefit you in some way.

It's not just about actions.

It's about vibrational alignment.

27
You're Always at a Crossroad

In every moment, you stand at a crossroad with only two directions to choose from: to feel good or to feel bad.

The choice is yours.

Your power to create your life also carries the responsibility of that creation. Just as you have the ability to create your worst nightmares, you also have the power to create your dream life.

This is the duality of the Universe.

It's easy to feel good when everything is going the way you want. But what about those moments when things don't unfold as you'd prefer? In these times, a powerful tool is to ask yourself: *"How is this benefiting me?"*

When you encounter a perceived "negative" experience, shifting your focus to how this situation could benefit you allows you to alchemize it into a positive one. You begin to explore how this experience might positively impact your growth, learning, or understanding. After all, everything is happening for your highest good, whether you can see it now or not. There are no accidents or coincidences.

Understanding that you hold the power to choose your response in every situation is the first step toward reclaiming control over your life.

**We are all alchemist of energy,
whether you're aware of it or not.**

28
Imagination: The Gateway to Creation

One cannot create without imagination.

> *"Logic will get you from A to B. Imagination will take you everywhere."*
>
> —Albert Einstein

As long as you can dream it, the Universe can serve it.

Decide what you want, and the Universe will conspire in your favor to deliver it.

Your subconscious mind cannot distinguish between what you see in your reality and what you imagine in your mind's eye. Going back to the idea that what you focus on, think about, and speak about is what you bring about—what you visualize in your mind, you will attract into your experience.

Remember, you only need to decide what your desires

are, imagine yourself in the end state, and feel the emotions you would experience if it were already real. The "how" or "when" doesn't matter; that's the job of the Universe. Therefore, hold no rigid expectations about how things will unfold and surrender to the magic of the Universe.

The truth is, there are no limits to your imagination. Whatever you can conceive in your mind, the Universe can serve up to you if you allow it.

Practice daydreaming, and visualize something that excites you. Even engaging with content related to your dreams can help. Play out the perfect scenario in your mind.

Spend five minutes today imagining your dream life in vivid detail. Allow yourself to be fully immersed in the experience:

- When you wake up in the morning, what do you see?
- What does your home look like?
- How do you feel?
- What kind of body do you have?
- What's the schedule of your day like?
- Do you have any cars? What do they look like?

- Do you own a boat or yacht? What does it look like?
- What's the dynamic within your family?

Imagine your dream life with as many details as possible! The more specific you get, the more powerful your visualization becomes. This exercise should feel fun and exciting, not like a chore. Allow yourself to enjoy the process and let your imagination run wild. The goal is to create a vivid picture of your desires that feels so real, it excites you every time you think about it.

If you find it challenging to visualize an image in your mind, start with something more tangible, like watching a video online about something you love. For example, if you've always dreamed of flying first class on a plane but can't imagine what it would be like, why not watch a video of someone else experiencing that? This way, you get a glimpse of what it's like, helping you imagine it for yourself.

As you imagine your dream life, focus on how each detail makes you feel. The stronger the emotions, the more magnetic your energy becomes.

Consistency is key, so make this visualization a part of your daily routine, and watch how your reality begins to shift in alignment with your dreams.

If others are capable of experiencing it, you are also capable of experiencing it too!

What you see in your mind's eye is a preview of what is to come. Recognize the power that comes with your imagination and the freedom that you possess. There is no such thing as being "too unrealistic." Don't let anyone tell you that your dream is too big or your desire too unattainable. If you can dream it, you can have it!

"The man who has no imagination has no wings."

—Muhammad Ali

29
Excitement Leads You to Alignment

This leads us to the well-known formula introduced by Bashar, channeled by Darryl Anka.

Bashar's Formula

1. **Act on your highest passion** (excitement, attraction, creativity).
2. **Act on it for as long as you can**, taking it as far as you can until you can take it no further.
3. **Take the actions without insistence or assumptions** about how the outcome should be.
4. **Stay in a positive state**, no matter what happens.
5. **Explore your belief system** and release any beliefs that no longer serve you.

The organizing principle of synchronicities will determine what happens in the next moment.

30
Patience

In the previous chapters, we explored the idea of surrendering to the flow of the Universe—trusting the process and allowing things to unfold naturally.

Patience often feels like a distant concept, something we're told to have but rarely understand how to cultivate. It's common to hear that we need faith and patience, yet these words can seem abstract, leaving us wondering how to genuinely embody them.

What does it mean to be patient? How do you find patience when you feel the urge to rush ahead?

The truth is, you only need patience when you feel impatience. Impatience arises when you're fixated on a future outcome, waiting for something better to arrive. But what if, instead of waiting, you chose to live fully in the present moment?

As Bashar teaches, when you follow your passion and excitement in every moment, when you do what lights you up, patience becomes unnecessary. There is no sense of waiting because you're so absorbed in the joy of what you're doing right now. In that state, you're not wishing to be somewhere else; you're not yearning for something more.

Impatience is born from the belief that something greater lies in the future, but in truth, there is nothing more valuable than the gift of this very moment. When you learn to appreciate the here and now, you release the need to be anywhere other than where you are.

Trust that everything unfolds in divine timing. The Universe's timing is always perfect.

When you embrace every experience as it comes, and when you choose to view each moment through a positive lens, you'll discover a new kind of freedom—the freedom that comes from knowing that right here, right now, is exactly where you are meant to be.

Patience isn't about waiting; it's about finding peace in the journey itself.

Everything unfolds in divine timing

31
Open All the Doors!

When you're faced with uncertainty, the best approach is to open all the doors. What does that mean? It means to explore every possibility that excites you—follow the threads of curiosity, passion, and inspiration. Don't limit yourself by thinking there's only one right path. Life is full of endless possibilities, and you are meant to explore them.

Some doors will close, and others will remain open. Instead of feeling discouraged when a door shuts, trust that it wasn't meant for you. A closed door is not a failure—it's guidance. The Universe, in its infinite wisdom, will always redirect you toward what aligns with your highest good.

It's like walking through a hallway of opportunities. Some paths will feel easy, others may feel blocked, and some might surprise you by opening wide just when you least expect it. Keep walking through the doors that open, knowing they are leading you exactly where you need to go.

Sometimes, you might be tempted to force a door open or grow frustrated when the path ahead isn't clear. In those moments, remember: what's meant for you will never pass you by. Trust the process, even if it's not unfolding the way you envisioned.

The Universe is always working in your favor, orchestrating things behind the scenes that you can't yet see. Every closed door is a step closer to the one that will open wide, welcoming you into new opportunities that are aligned with your highest good.

So, stay open, curious, and trusting. Explore. Take action. And when you feel a door click open, don't hesitate—step through with confidence, knowing that everything is always, always working out in your favor.

"When one door closes, another opens."

—Alexander Graham Bell

32
Feeling Anxious or Fearful? Here's What You Can Do.

To navigate uncertainty, cultivate self-trust.

When you don't know what to do, relax. Remind yourself that deeper parts of you do know.

Trust your higher self.

When you're in fear, tension builds. It's important to release that tension. It can be as simple as taking a deep breath, enjoying a bath in the ocean, getting a massage, or watching a comedy show. Choose whatever relaxes your body!

Since the mind and body are connected, how we feel physically can influence our mental state.

Fear often stems from the false belief that things aren't working out for you or that you aren't safe.

"Both faith and fear demand you to believe in something you cannot see. You choose."
—Bob Proctor

Remember, everything is working in your favor, whether you can see it or not. What if the things you cannot see now are all happening for you in ways you don't yet understand?

Trust yourself. Trust that your soul knows everything is as it should be. You are always in the right place at the right time. Your reading of this message is no accident.

"Doubt is not a lack of trust. It is a 100% trust in a negative belief that doesn't serve you."

—Bashar

33
When in Trouble, Call AAA

Bashar, channeled by Darryl Anka, offers a simple yet powerful strategy for navigating through difficulties or challenges. He calls it "Call AAA," which stands for:

1. **Acknowledge what you have, not what you don't have.**
2. **Appreciate what you have.**
3. **Allow what needs to come next.**

The essence of this approach lies in redirecting your attention away from what is missing in your life and focusing instead on what blessings you currently have. When you acknowledge what you have, you ground yourself in the present moment, shifting your awareness from lack to abundance.

Moving onto the next step, appreciation elevates your state of being. Gratitude has a high vibrational frequency that aligns you with positivity and openness, helping you maintain a clear connection to your inner wisdom and the guidance of the Universe. By focusing on gratitude, you ensure that fear, anxiety, or other lower states of mind don't derail you from your natural state of alignment.

Finally, the act of allowing means surrendering to the flow of life. Once you've acknowledged and appreciated what you have, you release control and trust that the Universe is unfolding as it should. This is where true growth happens. In this state of allowance, you open yourself up to receive new insights, opportunities, and solutions that you may not have seen before.

Remember, even when it doesn't seem clear in the moment, everything is always happening for your benefit. Challenges are often the catalysts for growth and transformation, guiding you to where you need to be.

"Spin everything to be positive because it always is!"

—Abraham Hicks

34
The Power of Water

This concept may be new to many in our modern society. A Japanese researcher and author, Masaru Emoto, conducted a series of experiments that explored the idea that water can absorb and retain the energy of thoughts, words, and feelings. Though we won't delve into the specifics of his experiments here, the key takeaway is this: because everything is energy, water has the ability to hold vibrational energy.

In other words, you can transmit your intentions, thoughts, words, or emotions into water, and this energetic information is then stored within it.

Considering that our bodies are made up of approximately 60% water, this concept becomes even more significant. Water can quickly penetrate to the cellular level, reaching the deepest parts of your body.

The idea is to set an intention for the water you drink or the water you use while showering. By doing so, you're infusing the water with a specific vibrational frequency that aligns with your intentions, which can then be absorbed deeply and quickly into your being. You can charge your water using spoken words, healing sound frequencies like solfeggio frequencies, music, or even crystals. The possibilities are limitless. You might program your water to hydrate your cells in the most optimal way, attract more love into your life, or increase your physical strength. The opportunities are endless, and it's up to you to choose the intentions you wish to set.

This understanding of water's potential allows you to become a true alchemist of energy, using this powerful element to help create your best life.

In everything you do, do it from your heart.

35
The Vibrational Frequencies of Fabrics

Believe it or not, every material has its own frequency, and different fabrics indeed possess unique vibrational energies. Now that you understand that your body has its own magnetic field, and that your thoughts and words are constantly shaping your reality, it's important to know that the fabric you wear can either enhance your energy or diminish it.

High vibrational frequencies have a positive impact on your well-being, while lower frequencies can have a negative effect.

Dr. Heidi Yellen's research has revealed that different fabrics have distinct vibrational frequencies that can influence the human body. For instance, natural fabrics like linen and wool have incredibly high vibrational frequencies—around 5,000 mHz, which is approximately 50 times higher than the average frequency of the human body. However, it's important to note that when linen and wool are worn together, they cancel out each other's frequencies.

Organic cotton has a vibrational frequency of about 100 mHz, which aligns well with the natural frequency of the human body, while non-organic cotton has a lower frequency of around 70 mHz.

On the other hand, synthetic fabrics and those treated with industrial chemicals tend to have much lower frequencies, comparable to the vibration of a person who is unwell or even that of a dead body.

Wearing high-frequency fabrics like linen, wool, organic cotton, and hemp can uplift you energetically, while synthetic fabrics can drain your energy due to their lower frequencies.

Being mindful of what you clothe your body with is another powerful way to raise your vibrational frequency and harness this energy to manifest your dreams.

I always get what I want, or better!

36
Money

We all seek abundance in our lives, and in today's world, money plays a key role in creating that sense of abundance. It's the primary means of exchanging value, giving us the freedom of time and choice. Money is a powerful tool that can empower you to shape your life. But how can you manifest more of it?

We've already discussed the power of imagination, the impact of your thoughts, words, and feelings, and the importance of removing limiting beliefs that block you from feeling worthy of receiving from the Universe. This inner work lays the foundation for attracting abundance into your life.

But let's get more specific—how does money actually flow into your life?

Money, at its core, is energy. It's a form of stored value, and like all forms of energy, it abides by the universal law that what you put out is what you get back. For money, value, or energy to flow into your life, you must first send out money, value, or energy into the world.

So, how do you put out money, value, or energy in a way that invites abundance back to you?

One key element is the frequency you emit when you think about or interact with money. Your relationship with money matters. Do you speak positively about money, or do you fear it? Do you view money through a lens of scarcity, or do you see it as a tool of empowerment and possibility? How you feel when you use money influences how money flows back to you.

Rev. Ike, a well-known spiritual teacher, offered a powerful tip: never use the word "spend" when talking about money. When you say you "spend" money, it implies that it's gone, never to return. Instead, replace the word "spend" with "circulate" or "use." You circulate money because it always returns to you in a flow. You use money as a tool to create the experiences you desire. The language you use shapes your relationship with money and directly affects your financial reality.

Just like water, money needs to flow. Stagnant water becomes unhealthy, and the same principle applies to money. When you cling to money out of fear or hold onto it without purpose, you disrupt its natural flow. While it's wise to save and be responsible, it's equally important to allow money to move, grow, and circulate. The more you let it flow, the more it returns to you. This doesn't mean spending recklessly, but rather understanding that money, as energy, thrives on movement and purpose.

Beyond your mindset, let's explore what else you can do to attract more money into your life.

If what you put out is what you get back, then to attract an abundant amount of wealth, you need to provide an abundant amount of value. The key lies in your passions and excitement. Each of us has unique talents, gifts, and a sense of purpose. When you follow what excites you the most, when you pour your energy into what lights you up, the natural outcome will be of value to others. Your passion will naturally lead you to create something that benefits those around you.

The more value you bring into the world, the more value the world will bring back to you. By pouring your energy into what you love, you create a ripple effect that enriches others, and as a result, money flows into your life as a reflection of that contribution.

Money is a mirror of your energy, your intentions, and the value you create. When you understand its true nature and let it flow freely, you align with the infinite potential of abundance that the Universe has to offer.

"You don't attract what you are worth, you attract what you believe you're worth."

—Rochelle Fox

37
Grounding and Healing

Everything is energy. Your physical body is made up of pure vibrational frequencies expressing themselves in the form you see in this 3-dimensional world. When you understand this, you realize that all disease (dis-ease) is simply a manifestation of frequencies that have fallen out of sync or become disharmonized. Your body, like a sponge, absorbs and stores energy from your surroundings and from every interaction you have. If these energies are not positively uplifting, they can weigh you down, disrupting your natural balance.

The food you consume also plays a crucial role in your energetic well-being. Each type of food carries its own frequency, which affects your body at the deepest energetic levels. In addition, modern life exposes us to toxins from various sources, from the air we breathe to the products we use, all of which can impact our body's energy.

One of the simplest yet most powerful ways to harmonize your body's energy is through grounding. Just as electrical appliances require grounding to stabilize their energy and prevent overload, your body needs the same connection to Mother Earth to release excess energy and restore balance. Grounding allows you to reconnect with the Earth's natural frequency, which can help reduce inflammation, release stress, and restore your inner equilibrium.

Stepping barefoot onto the earth, whether it's grass, soil, or sand, is a direct way to ground yourself. This practice can be scientifically measured by observing a significant change in your body's electrical charge before and after grounding. You can also extend this experience by using grounding mats or bed sheets, which allow you to stay connected to the Earth's energy even when you're indoors. Bathing in the ocean or simply placing your hands on a tree also offers powerful grounding effects, as trees are deeply connected to the Earth's electrical grid and act as natural conduits for grounding.

Sound frequencies are another profound way to restore harmony within your body. Healing frequencies, also known as sound therapy, have the ability to affect your mind and body at a cellular level. Unlike background music that just soothes the mind, these frequencies penetrate deep into your cells, promoting healing and realignment. Different frequencies serve unique purposes, from enhancing relaxation to accelerating physical and emotional recovery. Incorporating sound healing into your daily routine can be a transformative journey that elevates your overall well-being.

"The future medicine will be the medicine of frequencies."

—Albert Einstein

38
A Never-Ending Journey

You've made it! Take a moment to truly feel proud of yourself for taking this leap of faith and embarking on a transformative journey. Thank you for allowing me to share the inspirations and wisdom the Universe has revealed to me. I'm deeply grateful to be part of your path, helping you rediscover the magic within that empowers you to live each day fully.

As you move forward, may you embrace life from a new perspective—one filled with excitement, joy, and boundless possibilities. Remember, each day holds the potential for miracles, and you are the creator of your reality.

May you find peace and ease in living in flow, aligning your actions with your passions, and trusting the guidance of your higher self. Know that you are always loved, always supported, and never alone on this journey.

This journey doesn't end here. It's an ongoing, limitless adventure. Trust it, embrace it, and savor the magic that lies ahead.

Most importantly, never forget—the answers, the power, the transformation—all of it is within you, waiting to be lived and expressed.

Never forget, ***you are the magic***.

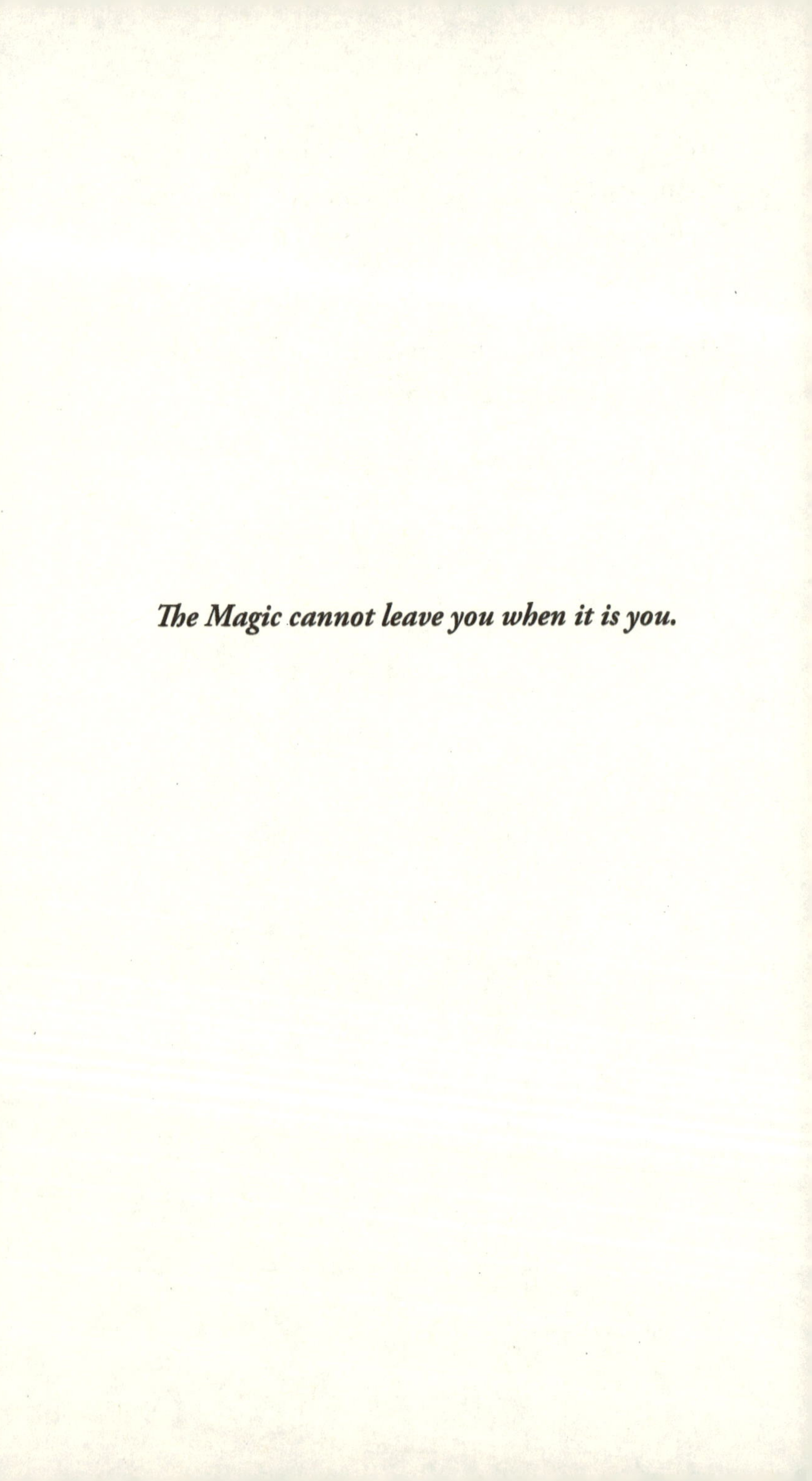

The Magic cannot leave you when it is you.

www.ingramcontent.com/pod-product-compliance
Lightning Source LLC
La Vergne TN
LVHW090528110826
845146LV00003B/1021

* 9 7 9 8 9 9 1 8 9 6 6 2 7 *